Voices for Green Choices

John Muir

Protecting and Preserving the Environment

By Henry Elliot

Crabtree Publishing Company

Crabtree Publishing Company

Author: Henry Elliot
Publishing plan research and development:
  Sean Charlebois, Reagan Miller
  Crabtree Publishing Company
Editor: Lynn Peppas
Proofreader: Crystal Sikkens
Project coordinator: Robert Walker
Content and curriculum adviser: Suzy Gazlay, M.A.
Editorial: Mark Sachner
Photo research: Ruth Owen
Design: Westgraphix/Tammy West
Production coordinator: Margaret Amy Salter
Prepress technicians: Margaret Amy Salter, Ken Wright

Written, developed, and produced by Water Buffalo Books

Cover photo: Breathtaking views such as this one of Yosemite National Park influenced President Theodore Roosevelt, an ally of John Muir, in how he viewed the environment and helped convince him to establish five U.S. national parks.

Photo credits:
Alamy: Tom Gardner: page 11 (bottom); Jiri Rezac: page 40 (left)
Corbis: Connie Rica: page 6 (left); Jonathan Blair: page 37 (top); Bettmann: page 38 (bottom)
FLPA: Tim Fitzharris: page 8 (bottom); Paul Hobson: page 11 (right); L Lee Rue: page 34 (top); STELLA: page 39 (right)
Getty Images: MPI: page 16 (left); Tod Korol: page 36 (bottom)
John Muir's Birthplace: page 13 (right)

High Sierra Volunteer Trail Crew: page 33 (left)
Holt-Atherton Special Collections, University of the Pacific Library. John Muir Papers. Copyright 1984 Muir-Hanna Trust: MuirFiche2Frame0080: page 5 (right); f24-1305: page 7 (bottom left); f23-1252: page 12 (bottom); MuirFiche4Frame0184: page 17 (bottom right); f23-1247: page 18 (left); MuirReel23Journal01P088-089: page 25 (bottom); Shone1.3.1.2: page 25 (right); f24-1349: page 27 (bottom); MSS305.1.3.3.1.4: page 28 (top); Shone1.3.1.6: page 30 (top); MuirFiche5Frame0282: page 30 (bottom); f25-1379: page 31 (bottom)
Courtesy of the Library of Congress: Image 3b00011u: front cover (inset); Image 3b00011u: page 1; Image 3g04698u: page 5 (bottom left); Image 3b43690u: page 7 (right); Image 3b00011u: page 8 (top left); Image 6a19572u: page 32 (top); Courtesy National Park Service, Museum Management Program and John Muir National Historic Site, California; Commemorative Envelope "John Muir: American Naturalist" with Stamp: JOMU 4261 B: page 41 (top right)
Alastair Seagrott: page 9 (left)
Shutterstock: front cover main; pages 4 (left), 10 (left), 14 ,15, 17 (top left), 20 (left), 22, 23, 24 (left), 26 (left), 27 (right), 28 (bottom), 31 (top), 32 (bottom), 34 (top right), 35, 39 (bottom), 42 (bottom)
Sierra Club: map of 1,000 mile walk: page 21 (top right)
Superstock: pages 13 (bottom), 21 (bottom)
United States Mint Image: page 41 (center right)
Wikipedia Creative Commons Attribution ShareAlike 2.5 licence: page 42 (top)
Wisconsin Historical Society: WHi-40625: page 17 (top right); WHi-10983: page 19 (right)

Library and Archives Canada Cataloguing in Publication

Elliot, Henry
    John Muir : protecting and preserving the environment / Henry Elliot.

(Voices for green choices)
Includes index.
ISBN 978-0-7787-4668-3 (bound).--ISBN 978-0-7787-4681-2 (pbk.)

    1. Muir, John, 1838-1914--Juvenile literature. 2. Naturalists--United States--Biography--Juvenile literature. 3. Conservationists--United States--Biography--Juvenile literature. 4. Environmentalists--United States--Biography--Juvenile literature. I. Title. II. Series: Voices for green choices

QH31.M9E45 2009   j333.72092   C2008-907977-9

Library of Congress Cataloging-in-Publication Data

Elliot, Henry.
  John Muir : protecting and preserving the environment / by Henry Elliot.
      p. cm. -- (Voices for green choices)
  Includes index.
  ISBN 978-0-7787-4681-2 (pbk. : alk. paper)
-- ISBN 978-0-7787-4668-3 (reinforced library binding : alk. paper)
  1. Muir, John, 1838-1914--Juvenile literature. 2. Naturalists--United States--Biography--Juvenile literature. 3. Conservationists--United States--Biography--Juvenile literature. 4. Environmentalists--United States--Biography--Juvenile literature. I. Title. II. Series.

  QH31.M9E55 2009
  333.72092--dc22
  [B]
                                                    2008053024

Crabtree Publishing Company

www.crabtreebooks.com   1-800-387-7650

Published in Canada
Crabtree Publishing
616 Welland Ave.
St. Catharines, Ontario
L2M 5V6

Published in the United States
Crabtree Publishing
PMB16A
350 Fifth Ave., Suite 3308
New York, NY 10118

Published in the United Kingdom
Crabtree Publishing
White Cross Mills
High Town, Lancaster
LA1 4XS

Published in Australia
Crabtree Publishing
386 Mt. Alexander Rd.
Ascot Vale (Melbourne)
VIC 3032

Contents

Chapter 1

The President Goes Camping

May, 1903. It was a chilly night in Yosemite National Park, high in California's Sierra Nevada. Two men sat close to a crackling campfire. It could be a scene like any other camping trip of two good friends—except that one of these men was Teddy Roosevelt, the president of the United States. The other was John Muir.

Two Legendary Figures

As soon as they entered the park, Roosevelt was overcome by the view, and he asked Muir to show him the real Yosemite. They talked late into the night and were awakened by snow dust in the morning. It was a trip Roosevelt never would forget.

Of all the events in the life of John Muir, his camping trip with President Roosevelt is the best known. Think of it! The president of the United States camping deep in the rugged wilderness of Yosemite with a scraggly looking mountain man. The two men brought along five mules and a cook, but even though the previous president had been assassinated just two years earlier, Roosevelt would not allow his Secret Service agents to come along. For three days and two nights, President Roosevelt had no contact with the United States government. His only companion was John Muir.

▲ Breathtaking views of Yosemite influenced President Theodore Roosevelt and his conservation policies. An ally of John Muir, Roosevelt would help establish five United States national parks.

By the time John Muir camped with the president, he was already one of America's most influential naturalists. Roosevelt had read John Muir's 1901 book, *Our National Parks*, and it left a deep impression on him. Unlike other nature writers, John Muir did not just describe his experiences in the wilderness. He passionately argued for passage of laws to protect the wilderness. In 1892 he founded an organization, the Sierra Club, "to make the mountains glad," and to keep canyons, giant trees, and hillsides pure and uncontaminated. Other nature writers of his time were known as naturalists or conservationists. Muir was a preservationist who fought to keep nature pure and safe from the influence of people.

Speaking Up for Mother Nature

Muir used this camping trip to tell the president about California's mismanagement of the Yosemite Valley and of the danger to the valley's resources. He did his best to convince Roosevelt that the best way to protect the valley was through federal

"Climb the mountains and get their good tidings. Nature's peace will flow into you as sunshine flows into trees. The winds will blow their own freshness into you, and the storms their energy, while cares will drop off like autumn leaves."

- John Muir, *Our National Parks* (1901)

▲ Both a sketch artist and a nature writer, John Muir filled his notebooks with images of the landscapes he explored. Above is the Kings River as it flows through Yosemite.

◀ United States President Theodore Roosevelt (left), a great outdoorsman, and John Muir, founder of the Sierra Club, camped together in the Sierra Nevada in 1903.

5

control and management, and he succeeded. This was a key moment for Muir, for Roosevelt, and for the American people. Roosevelt would go on to establish 148 million acres (60 million hectares) of national forest, five national parks, and 23 national monuments during his term of office.

Certainly, long before John Muir camped with Teddy Roosevelt, and long before the arrival of

Europeans, Native people in the Americas had marked hundreds of protected places. These were known as sacred burial and holy grounds. Spirit Mound in South Dakota and Chickasawba Mound in Arkansas are just two. But European settlers soon forged their own culture, values, and ways of life in the Americas. Progress in the nineteenth century took on a life of its own. Many great things were achieved to give Americans opportunities available nowhere else in the world. Preserving American wilderness, however, was not among those achievements.

▲ Native Americans routinely recognized some nature areas as "off limits" to hunting and settlement. Spirit Mound, above, is one of many hundreds of Native holy grounds.

Up until John Muir, much of the history of the United States had been one of conquering nature and, even more horrifyingly, conquering the people closest to nature. The buffalo, the passenger pigeon, the forests and lakes, and Native Americans— nothing stood in the way of "progress" and the move West. But as John Muir walked the wilderness of the United States and other parts of the world, something began to change. He documented his adventures and turned his journals into books and magazine articles. He met face to face with two United States presidents. Looking back, it was the beginnings of today's environmental movement, and the planting of the seeds of controversy surrounding offshore drilling, global warming, and other issues.

A Founding Activist

Is John Muir "The Father of Our National Parks," as he is so often called? This title is somewhat misleading. Many other writers and politicians joined him in his campaign to protect the American wilderness. Along with writers Henry David Thoreau and John Burroughs, businessman Edward Henry Harriman, and presidents Grover Cleveland, Teddy Roosevelt, and William Howard Taft, Muir was certainly one

Edward Henry Harriman, Railroad Baron and Friend of Nature

E. H. Harriman was a lifelong naturalist and friend of John Muir. A wealthy railroad baron, he owned five railroads and a few other companies. In 1899 he financed a voyage aboard a luxury steamship to Canada so that Muir and others could study plant and animal life along the Alaskan coast. In 1912, John Muir published Harriman's biography, praising him for his efforts to protect North America's wilderness.

▲ John Muir's work was supported by Edward Henry Harriman, shown here with his wife.

◀ John Muir never rushed when exploring nature. He stopped often to record his observations and thoughts in great detail. His notebooks have provided much information for this book.

▲ Although John Muir studied geology, engineering, and botany, his love of nature was more spiritual than scientific.

▼ Thanks to the lifelong efforts of John Muir, people today can still enjoy vistas in Yosemite and elsewhere in all their natural splendor.

of the founding fathers, and his voice still echoes loud and clear from Florida to Alaska and beyond.

John Muir was a rambunctious child, inventor, wanderer, geologist, botanist, writer, family man, friend of presidents, political lobbyist, vehement advocate for the preservation of America's wilderness, the original Mountain Man, and living symbol of the environmentalist movement. As an activist, John did not always win. His very last battle—to save Hetch Hetchy Valley in Yosemite from being dammed up and flooded—failed. Even in defeat, however, John Muir left a legacy that inspires many to protect the environment and to make his fight their own.

This is the story of John Muir, and how his life became a movement.

Chapter 2

Boyhood in Scotland and Wisconsin

On the grounds of a crumbling castle near their home, little John Muir and his brother David picked up small branches. These were their swords. Running and jumping amid the ruins, the brothers made believe they were gallant Scottish soldiers defeating the English army in a famous 1300s battle known to all Scotsmen.

A Boyhood Filled with Adventure

Growing up in Scotland, John had no shortage of brothers and sisters to play with. When he wasn't re-enacting famous battles from Scottish history that he learned about in school, John and his brothers and friends would hold contests to see who could find the most birds' nests in the fields and woods around their homestead.

John Muir was born on April 21, 1838, and he lived in Scotland until 1849, when his family moved to Wisconsin in the United States. His parents, Daniel Muir and Ann Gilrye, had seven children born in Scotland, three boys and four girls, and another girl after they emigrated to the United States.

Young John Muir would never lose the thrill of bird watching, but as he grew into the naturalist he was to become, he would give up the practice of collecting the nests

▲ This statue, which stands on High Street near John Muir's birthplace in Dunbar, Scotland, shows him as a boy out in nature. Dunbar has become a popular attraction for people who want to see the places where John had many of his childhood adventures.

> *"Surely all God's people, however serious or savage, great or small, like to play. Whales and elephants, dancing, humming gnats, and invisibly small mischievous microbes . . . [all] must have lots of fun in them."*
>
> - John Muir, *The Story of My Boyhood and Youth* (1913)

▼ The rocky coast of the North Sea provided a wild, and often treacherous, place for John to observe marine life in its natural habitat. Later in life, John would write that the wildness of the sea and woods got into his blood.

unless they were abandoned. And even though he soon outgrew swordplay, in a sense he would become another kind of warrior, a proud American fighting a lifelong battle to preserve nature and the environment against those who threatened it.

Wildness in His Blood

Daniel Muir was a very strict father, and John was a very rebellious son. Dunbar, where they lived, was near the North Sea, where waves crashed on the rocks and strange sea life washed up on the shores. When he wasn't scampering in the woods and brambled fields, John searched for eels and crabs on the dangerous shore. Although his father insisted that John play close to home in the gated garden, John just wouldn't, or couldn't, obey. Each time he got caught, he would be harshly punished, but even this didn't stop him. As a seven-year-old, John was already a rebel.

A Favorite Haunt

Another favorite playground was Dunbar Castle. It was overgrown, crumbling, and more than one thousand years old. There John and his playmates climbed, jumped, ran, and exercised their boyish energies despite the perils of occasional accidents.

In the 1800s in Scotland, and even today, stories of ghosts and witches were told among children and passed down from older to younger. The stories were

often told to frighten young children into good behavior: "Don't go climbing at Dunbar Castle or the ghosts will get you." But with John, this tactic backfired, and he only practiced his jumping, running, and climbing skills even more so he could escape the witches and ghosts.

More Than Just Fun and Games

John's childhood was not all adventure and play. In the 1840s, school in Scotland was rigorous. By the age of eight or nine, students took Latin and French classes as well as the more familiar studies in English, spelling, history, arithmetic, and geography. John spoke Scots, but he soon learned English, Latin, and French grammar by heart. And because Daniel Muir was so religious, he also insisted that his son study the Bible. By age 11, John had almost the entire Bible memorized.

During John's boyhood in Scotland, typical Muir family meals were not very tasty. Breakfast was

◀▲ Dunbar Castle was first built over 1,000 years ago as a defense against English invaders. Today, the castle ruins seem in places to be part of the natural landscape. The castle stones provide a nesting place for many seabirds (above), whose eggs John would have prized as a young boy. **11**

At Home with English and Scottish

Once he moved to the United States, John Muir became an articulate speaker and writer of English. His first language was Scottish, and this was the language he spoke as a young boy in his home, in school, and at play. The Scottish language is both close to, and different from, English.

Here are a few examples of Scottish words and their meanings in English:

English	Scottish
children	bairn
did not	dinna
have	hae
dare	daur
know	ken
mother	mither
America	Amaraka
joking	haverin
brook	burn
a scare	fleg
beautiful	bonnie

usually oatmeal. Lunch, which was called dinner, consisted of some vegetable broth, a biscuit made from ground barley, and a small piece of boiled mutton, which is meat from sheep. The Muir children's after-school snack, which was called "tea," consisted of a half slice of bread without butter and a drink made of water, milk, and sugar. Supper was the last meal of the day and usually featured a boiled potato and another barley biscuit. After supper, there were never late-night snacks. There was only time for family worship, then off to bed.

Shocking News

One evening in 1849, when John was 11, his father told him and his brother David to put away their studies because the next morning they were leaving for the "New World." With just one day's notice, the boys were shocked. Yet John felt nothing but pure joy. He had heard about North America, about its birds and forests, and he imagined it as a place with no schools, or stern groundskeepers.

► As an adult, John Muir wrote about his childhood fascination with the natural world.

This would be the best adventure of his life. Little did he know how right and wrong he would be. At first, only his father Daniel, his 13-year-old sister Sarah, John, and his nine-year-old brother David would go. John's mother, Ann, and his younger siblings

Margaret, Daniel Jr., Mary, and Anna would stay behind until Daniel could build a new family homestead.

The next morning, four members of the Muir family set off across the Atlantic on a long sea voyage to the United States.

Once in the United States, John and his brother, sister, and father made their way to Wisconsin. John's father quickly found land on a sunny lakeside for his new farm. John and David immediately found the trees and skies around the farm filled with jays, hawks, cranes, kingbirds, woodpeckers, and many other bird species. They also marveled at the frogs, snakes, fireflies, and many trees, plants, and flowers they had never seen before. They couldn't have been more excited.

A Hard, Productive Life

But John, David, and Sarah did not come all the way to America just to enjoy the charms of nature. As the oldest daughter, Sarah took on the

▲ Although John died a wealthy man, the Muir family home in Scotland was very humble, and the Muirs had very little income.

◀ Like many Europeans in the 1800s, John's father Daniel sought to improve his family's fortunes by sailing to America on a ship like this. John was 11 at the time.

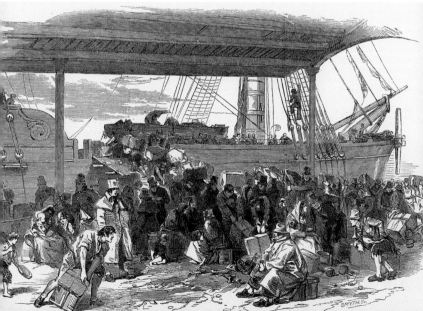

13

American Robin

Bobolink

Belted Kingfisher

Field Sparrow

Wisconsin Birds Near and Far

There are hundreds of birds that are native to Wisconsin. Wisconsin birds migrate and have far-ranging territories and can be spotted in many other areas as well. John Muir saw most of these birds in one season or another. Here are a few species of rare and common birds.

cooking and other household chores, and John and his brother were there to help with the equally hard work of clearing the land and building the house. Work was especially difficult in the harsh winters, when it was John's responsibility to care for the work horses and feed the livestock with heavy baskets of Indian corn. One summer, it was John's job to chisel a 90-foot- (27-meter-) deep well on the family farm. It took him all summer, but he did it. Work like this helped John grow into a strong, self-disciplined young man.

The farm house was built by autumn, and the family was reunited soon after that. Corral, barn, and fences were also put up, and the family farm soon had chickens, pigs, cows, oxen, and a pony. Compared to their rough-hewn life in rocky Scotland, they prospered on their Wisconsin farm.

At Home in Nature

As the months passed, John's observation skills

14 Wild Turkey

Red-headed Woodpecker

Scarlet Tanager

Great Horned Owl

grew keen. He soon knew almost every species of bird in Wisconsin. He knew what season they arrived in their migrations and when they headed south. He learned to recognize bird species just by hearing their song, and he could mimic their calls. By the time he was 13, John Muir was an amateur ornithologist with an encyclopedic knowledge of birds.

When John talked about birds, it was not an encyclopedia of cold facts. He spoke of them in a way that showed a true affection. He described the common robin in his memoirs as follows: "None of the bird people of Wisconsin welcomed us more heartily than the common robin. Far from showing alarm at the coming of settlers into their native woods, they reared their young around our gardens as if they liked us, and how heartily we admired the beauty and fine manners of these graceful birds and their loud cheery song of 'Fear not, fear not, cheer up, cheer up.' It was easy to love them."

Different Attitudes from Today

For the Muirs, as for other settlers in the 1800s, family life differed from our lives today in many ways. This was no less true of the Muirs. Because roles for boys and girls were so different, John's sisters rarely joined him in his countryside adventures. Instead, girls were restricted to activity in the home and hardly ever wandered beyond the garden.

John's father loved his son, but Daniel was also a strict disciplinarian. When John disobeyed and got caught, it meant physical punishment. If John could not resist playing in the fields and neglected his chores, his

Be an Amateur Ornithologist
Ask your librarian to help you find a book about birds in your state or province. Or try an Internet search using "(your state) birds." Then ask a parent to take you and a few other classmates to a nearby nature park or reserve, and keep a checklist of how many of your state's birds you can see and identify.

▲ The common robin can be found in almost every state. Its appearance is often an early sign of spring. Robins were one of young John's favorite birds.

father would spank him with a "switch," a long, thin branch of a willow tree. Those punishments might sound harsh today, but at the time such spankings were considered "normal."

The Muir family met their first Native North Americans in the middle of the 1800s, when non-Native attitudes and United States government policies were cruel toward Native people. Occasionally, Menominee and Winnebago people would stop by the Muir home, and the Muirs would invite them to sharpen their knives on the family grindstone. At the same time, the family was suspicious of Native ways, and they watched their visitors closely to make sure they did not sneak off with their horse or some chickens. Despite this distrust, John marveled at their knowledge of animals and especially their hunting skills. During their Wisconsin years, John and his brothers often saw deer tracks, but a deer usually saw them before they spied it, so they would rarely get close enough to get a good look. Much to his amazement and admiration, Native Americans could silently stalk deer on foot.

▲ Menominee Natives lived and hunted in the lands near the Muir farm. John was fascinated with their knowledge of the wilderness and their hunting abilities.

A Spirit in Tune with Nature

During his Wisconsin years, John began to develop more than just a sharp mind that observed nature. He began to sense spirituality in nature. It was in the woods, not in church or at family worship, where John felt he "heard" his finest sermons. He had a feeling that everything in nature was connected. This feeling would grow stronger throughout his life.

▲ John and his brothers became very skilled at spotting birds and most woodland animals. Deer were the hardest for them to see. The boys had not mastered the skill of moving quietly and unseen.

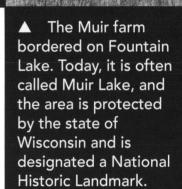

▲ The Muir farm bordered on Fountain Lake. Today, it is often called Muir Lake, and the area is protected by the state of Wisconsin and is designated a National Historic Landmark.

During his 11 years in Wisconsin, John never roamed more than 15 miles (24 km) from his home. But those 15 miles were 15 miles of discovery, and something special happened to John Muir. It happened in short bits of time, maybe 30 minutes before starting his chores, or a few minutes when he could sneak away from his chores, or for whole hours on Sundays.

It was during these times that John changed. His ability to observe the wildlife around grew keener than anyone around him. His admiration for nature soared to a level of religion. He opened his heart and mind to the wonders of life in the natural world in a way few other people have before or since. He was destined for great things.

▶ Young John Muir's sketch of the family cabin erected soon after their arrival in Wisconsin in 1849.

The Bur-oak shanty. Wisconsin

Chapter 3

John Muir finished up his time in Wisconsin by attending school for several years at the University of Wisconsin in Madison. He then went to Canada briefly before the next big event in his life: walking 1,000 miles (1,600 km) from Indiana to Florida.

An Ingenious Youth

Unlike his very early years in Scotland, John hardly attended school at all while living at the farm. This did not mean that young John did not hunger for knowledge. He wanted to read as much as he could despite the objections of his deeply religious father. Daniel Muir believed that the only book a boy needed to read was the Bible. Still, whenever he could, John smuggled books into the home and hid them in his room.

At the age of 15, John turned his energies to studying math and inventing curious gadgets and contraptions. His clocks were especially ingenious. Using scrap metal and wood, John made an outdoor clock so large it could be seen by field workers hundreds of yards away. He also invented an alarm clock. This clock worked with a simple bed, and when the alarm went off, it would dump the sleeper from the bed to the floor! No hitting the snooze button on that one.

▲ John Muir as he looked around the time he began his life-changing 1,000-mile (1,600 km) walk. In 1867 he walked all the way from Indiana to Florida.

At about the time that John was reading and inventing things on his own, he decided to enroll at the University of Wisconsin. He took botany classes because he wanted to learn about plant life, but he did not keep track of class credits or work toward a degree. While he was studying there, the United States was in the grips of the great Civil War, and tents for wounded soldiers were set up on parts of the campus. John was a pacifist. He called war the "most infernal of all civilized calamities." The sight of horribly wounded soldiers made him even more anti-war than ever.

"Wander a whole summer if you can. Thousands of God's blessings will search you and soak you as if you were a sponge, and the big days will go by uncounted."

- *John of the Mountains: The Unpublished Journals of John Muir* (first published 1938, University of Wisconsin Press)

From Wisconsin to Ontario

Though John was not drafted into the Union army, he probably knew that was a possibility, and in 1864 he left Wisconsin and went to Canada. John knew the Trout family because they belonged to the same church as the Muirs. The Trouts ran a sawmill in southeast Ontario. What started out as a short visit turned into a two-year stay. John became friends with the two Trout brothers and had a flirty romance with their sister, Harriet. During his time with the Trouts, John used his skills as a mechanical inventor to improve the running of their mill. He redesigned pulleys and rearranged gears. By the time he finished tinkering, the sawmill was turning out twice as many broom and rake handles.

John Muir also used his stay in Ontario to put his botany studies to use. He walked around the perimeter of Lake

▲ Muir's most bizarre clock was one he invented for college students. When it was time to wake up, the clock would light the fireplace and a study lamp. Then it would open a book for the student to read.

Huron to identify and catalog as many plants as he could. Later in his life, Muir would write that he was leaving "the University of Wisconsin for the University of the Wilderness" and these walks in Canada were his freshman year. It was during these walks that he learned the endurance and skills he would need to survive his legendary 1,000-mile (1,600-km) walk. Often he would have little to eat. At other times he was not prepared for the cold nights, and once he was threatened by wolves. The next year he published his first newspaper article, a piece on a rare plant he discovered in the Great Lakes region.

John Muir loved the wilds of Ontario; he liked the Trouts, especially Harriet, and he considered settling down there. But when the Trout sawmill burned to the ground in 1866, fate took a hand.

An Ambitious Plan

Returning to the United States, John began to hatch an ambitious plan. He proposed to walk to Florida, then sail to Cuba, walk through Cuba, take a boat to South America, and walk through South America. The route he mapped out would have taken him through the dangerous Amazon jungles. It never happened quite that way, however. After arriving in Florida, Muir became very ill, probably with malaria, and his recovery left him too weak to carry out his plan. John never fully abandoned his dream though, and he finally made it happen with a trip to South America 44 years later!

Before starting his journey, John knew he would need money for food, lodging, and occasional travel by steam ship or train. He took a job as an engineer

▼ John's first newspaper article, "The Calypso Borealis," told of his walks around the Great Lakes and in particular of how he discovered a rare orchid there.

Sauntering

For a man who walked as much as he did, John Muir hated to hike. For John, "hiking" meant rushing and not stopping to observe. He preferred to "saunter" at a more leisurely pace so he could appreciate as much around him as his senses could absorb.

at a factory in Indianapolis, Indiana, where he was very successful. In March of 1867, a terrible factory accident injured his eyes, and for many weeks he was blind. Luckily, he recovered his sight after two months. If his success at engineering ever tempted him to make a career of it, this accident was the final push away from the cities and into the wilderness.

In early September 1867, at the age of 29, he set off. He headed south toward the tip of Florida. This walk took him about two months. He averaged 17 miles (27 km) a day.

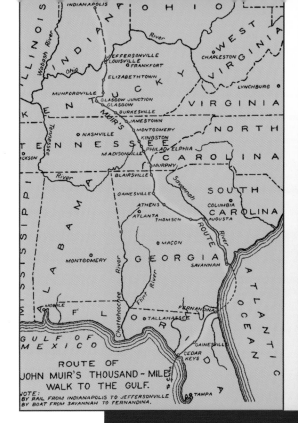

ROUTE OF JOHN MUIR'S THOUSAND - MILE WALK TO THE GULF.

NOTE: BY RAIL FROM INDIANAPOLIS TO JEFFERSONVILLE BY BOAT FROM SAVANNAH TO FERNANDINA.

A Tour of the South

John spent the first ten days of his trip south walking through Kentucky, where he found and explored many caves, including Mammoth Cave. The cave was already becoming a tourist attraction,

▲ John Muir's 1,000-mile walk took him on a meandering path from Indiana through Kentucky, Tennessee, Georgia, and ended in Florida. If John had had his way, he would have continued walking through Central and South America.

◄ Mammoth Cave in Kentucky was one of the many wonders that John Muir saw on his 1,000-mile walk. John's book about this experience would not be published until after his death, 50 years later!

21

▲ Mistletoe, which has become a "kissing" tradition for the Christmas and New Year holidays, is actually a parasite that can kill the trees in which it is found. John Muir observed and wrote about mistletoe while on his 1,000-mile walk.

▼ Until the railroads were built, the only way American settlers could cross west of Tennessee was through the Cumberland Gap. John walked through the rugged Gap on foot.

but Muir found Mammoth Cave far superior to the nearby hotel with its artificial gardens. It was in Kentucky too that Muir saw mistletoe, a tree parasite, for the first time.

As he crossed into Tennessee, Muir immediately took a path up the Cumberland Mountains, the first real mountains he had ever encountered. Halfway up, he looked back on the Kentucky forests of grand oak, walnut, hickory, and elm trees. The panorama took his breath away.

After 12 days in Tennessee, Muir entered Georgia. There Muir was exhilarated by the variety of fruits and plants he had never seen before. There were bananas, pomegranate fruit, bamboo, Spanish moss, and grassy swamps that were home to alligators. He also saw the scars of the Civil War that were still visible in the landscape and the people.

Throughout his 1,000-mile walk, John depended on the hospitality of strangers. He often passed a night and enjoyed an evening meal with generous farmers or townspeople. He met many former slaves and many former slave owners. He was grateful to both for their generosity. He was also impressed with the former slaves' keen knowledge of the forested lands and waters.

As John continued in the general direction of Savannah, Georgia, he encountered several challenges. He ran into swift river currents and rattlesnakes. More than once he was rudely washed downstream as he tried to ford a river.

And hospitality was sometimes hard to find. In the deeper South, plantation owners were often very leery of "Yankees." He frequently spent the night sleeping in the woods getting bitten by bugs. Even when he did sleep the night as someone's guest, when morning came John was always eager to get away from civilization and back to the wilderness.

He finally reached Savannah on October 8 but ran out of money. He stayed there several days and had to sleep in a cemetery until money from his brother arrived by wire. Then he traveled by boat to the northeast coast of Florida.

Florida at Last

Muir had fantasized so much about Florida that his first impression was a big letdown. Instead of a forest of flowering trees sparkling in the sunlight, what he saw first were salt marshes entangled in water vines. Instead of passing into a promised land, Muir felt lonely and out of place. But as he set off to cross Florida from east to west, he soon learned the wonders of plant life in the swampy everglades. Palm trees, magnolia trees, and

A "Thing" about Alligators

While crossing the Everglades, if John Muir heard a noise he would jerk his head and jump nervously. In his mind, he knew alligators were God's creatures. He also saw them as part of nature's divine plan and not as demons. But that didn't stop him from watching where he stepped.

◄ Once he reached Florida, John crossed the state through the Everglades, wading out into the swamps to collect plants.

Malaria

Malaria is a dangerous disease. During the building of the Panama Canal in the 1890s, malaria killed thousands of workers. Symptoms include fever, chills, headache, nausea, and vomiting. It can last months, and often it comes back in regular cycles. Malaria is transmitted to people when they are bitten by mosquitoes (below) that carry a malaria parasite, but this was not known until the 1890s. The disease is most common in the tropics and subtropics.

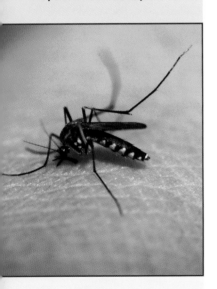

stands of wild lime particularly caught his attention.

Muir crossed the Everglades on a path created for railroad tracks and waded out into the murky waters left and right to examine and collect plant species. He often sank in the mud or got tangled in the reeds, and sometimes both.

Surviving the Everglades, Muir arrived in Gainesville, and from there he headed south to the Gulf of Mexico. His walk was nearly over, though he did not know it. He planned to sail to Cuba on the next cargo ship he could find. But instead, John took ill—very ill. Up to this point in his life, John Muir had been a picture of health. But now he suffered from a high persistent fever that left him delirious and lasted for almost three months. John Muir had malaria.

His recovery was slow, but one day in January, when he was feeling much better, a commercial sailing ship came into the town harbor, and Muir eagerly booked passage on it for a trip to Cuba.

On to Cuba

Cuba is only 100 miles (160 km) away from Cedar Key, where Muir was recovering, and the sea journey only took one full day. It was a rocky voyage. A fierce storm came up, and white foam waves splashed hard on the decks. The captain ordered Muir below, but he pleaded to stay on deck. The captain and the crew thought he must still be delirious, but for John the stormy sea and wild waves were a thrilling example of nature's beauty and harmony. Above deck he stayed.

The ship sailed into the Havana harbor, and John Muir saw old churches, town squares filled with flower gardens, bustling open-air markets tumbling with bananas, oranges, and pineapples (the first he had ever seen and tasted). For almost every traveler, these sights, sounds, and smells would seem like an exotic and exciting vacation, but John Muir was not any normal traveler. For John, the frequent peal of church bells, the music played in public squares, and the ceremonial cannon fire from the fort were all noise. His only thought was how to escape from Havana's confusion and get back to the pure heart of nature.

Malaria is a stubborn disease, and John was not free from its grip. His desire to go to the middle of the island and climb the interior mountains was simply not possible. Instead, he passed his days slowly zigzagging along the shore away from, but close by, the city. Even these modest saunters were great stores of discovery, and John collected many vines, flowers, and leaves, each one carefully pressed flat. Each evening, he returned to the ship for an evening meal, rest, and sleep.

Soon after that, John Muir booked passage on a ship to New York, then rode a train cross-country to California. A new beginning lay just ahead.

A "Thing" about Hunters

During this phase of his life, John Muir grew to dislike hunting and the attitudes of hunters. He criticized hunters for believing it was their right to track animals in the woods and kill them. John believed that a bear had every bit as much right to attack a person who trespassed in the bear's territory. "If a war of races should occur between the wild beasts and Lord Man," he wrote, "I would be tempted to sympathize with the bears."

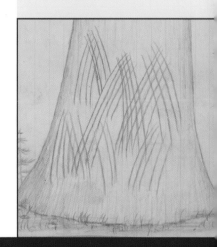

◀ ▲ Pages from the daily journal John Muir kept on his 1,000-mile walk. John combined notes and sketches in his journal. The sketch above, entitled "Bear Writing," reflects his interest in, and possibly his sympathy for, bears. **25**

Chapter 4

The California Years

In 1868, when John Muir was 30, he arrived in California. He thought he might stay for a year, just so he could look around the valleys while he fully recovered his health. Even though he would travel far and wide before his death in 1914, he called California home for the rest of his life. And here begins the next phase of his story.

During this time Muir traveled and wrote in abundance. He traveled through the Sierra Nevada of California, in Alaska, and throughout the world. He married and with his wife had two daughters. He would campaign successfully to save wilderness, and came to describe nature almost as if were a kind of Higher Power. And he would fight a fierce, but losing, "holy" battle to stop one dam, in particular, from being built.

The Majesty of Yosemite

One of the first things John did when he got to California was to visit the Yosemite Valley. What he saw surpassed all his expectations. Granite cliffs soared above multi-colored canyons and sparkling rivers and streams. He would later write, "No temple made of hands can compare with Yosemite." In these words John showed how nature was becoming his religion.

John had to eat, so he soon returned to the Sierra foothills and looked for work. At various

▲ Regal giant sequoia trees were among the first natural sights that greeted John when he settled in California. They typically grow to over 200 feet (60 m) tall. The oldest trees on record are about 3,200 years old. The tallest recorded tree is 311 feet (95 m).

times he found employment at a sawmill and as a ferryman and a shepherd. Each time he earned enough money he returned to Yosemite to climb its peaks, descend its trails, and think about this magnificent landscape and how it developed.

The common belief at the time was that Yosemite was formed by massive earthquakes. But Muir disagreed. His keen powers of observation and his creative imagination led him to the theory—since proven to be correct—that Yosemite was formed by glaciers and that its land was once iced over.

It was about this time that John began to edit his journals and publish magazine articles. Later he collected and expanded these articles and published them as books. At this time, too, his interests shifted from geology back to botany, especially giant sequoia trees.

Big Events

The year 1880 was a big one for John. Now 42 years old, he married Louisa Strentzel in April. It was a marriage that would last until Louisa

"Everybody needs beauty as well as bread, places to play in and pray in, where nature may heal and give strength to body and soul alike."

- John Muir, *The Yosemite* (1912)

▲ Although John Muir lived on the Strentzel family ranch, he felt more at home in Yosemite.

◄ John Muir with his wife, Louisa, and his daughters, Wanda and Helen.

Muir the Scribbler

John Muir (right) wrote more than 15 books and dozens of magazine articles. Here is a partial list of his more influential works:

• The Mountains of California (1894) was John Muir's first book. It contains a well-known and exciting story of how he climbed a tree and hung on for dear life during an all-night windstorm.

• *Our National Parks* (1901) was Muir's most influential book. He describes in vivid detail his walks in Yosemite, Sequoia, Yellowstone, Glacier, and other parks of the American West.

• *Stickeen* (1909) is a favorite with younger readers. It tells of John's adventures with his companion, a little dog, as they explore glaciers in Alaska.

• *The Yosemite* (1912) is Muir's travel guide to his favorite park.

• *The Story of My Boyhood & Youth* (1913) is Muir's autobiography of his first 20 years. It covers his boyhood in Scotland and Wisconsin.

• *A Thousand Mile Walk to the Gulf* (1916) is compiled from his nature journals. This book tells of John's walk from Indiana to Florida in the 1860s soon after the Civil War.

(or 'Louie,' as John called her) died in 1905.

Later in the summer of 1880, he traveled to Alaska, the second of his four Alaska trips. He brought a dog named Stickeen with him. One day, as the two were crossing a glacier, the weather turned dangerous. Their survival was in doubt. John wrote about their sharing courage, fear, true grit, and a respect for the storm that tried to kill them both. To John, he and the dog shared a holy experience on that glacier, and he felt a spiritual kinship with Stickeen unlike any other he had experienced.

In some ways, John's marriage to Louisa was an odd match. Louie was a liberated, independent woman. She was an accomplished musician and an

▲ Next to the Sierra Valley and Yosemite, the rugged wilderness of Alaska was John Muir's favorite exploring grounds. He made three trips there, identified hundreds of plant and animal species, and nearly lost his life in an arctic blizzard.

excellent manager of her family's thriving ranch. They had a daughter, Wanda, in 1881, and another, Helen, born in 1886. Both girls also studied music and became quite accomplished in their own right.

Louie didn't like camping or the wilderness, and domestic life cramped John's style. For eight years he did very little exploring. Instead, he worked on editing his notes and journals. While he explored the wilderness, he would take pages and pages of sloppy notes. Only later, often many years later, would he go back to these notes and polish them into a book manuscript. For example, his Alaska adventure with Stickeen in 1880 was not published as a book until 1909.

Being at home and away from nature was hard on John, and his health began to suffer. He handed over the responsibilities of raising the girls and managing the ranch to Louie and thrust himself back into the wilderness as much as possible. He was now 52.

A View All His Own

John traveled back to the Sierra Nevada and Alaska. He also walked the wilds of Europe, China, India, Australia, Indonesia, Hawaii, and more. In 1911, when he was 73, he even toured the wilderness of Africa and the Amazon Valley of South America!

John often spent time among Native Americans and First Nations (Canadian Indians) during his travels in the Sierra Nevada, Alaska, and Canada. In his journals he wrote about the Indians of California and of

Keep a Nature Journal

Keeping a nature journal is an excellent way to sharpen powers of observation and open eyes to many things in nature that are often taken for granted. John Muir kept nature journals his entire adult life. Afterward, when he wanted to write letters or essays, he'd use his journals for inspiration. Here is how you can follow in John Muir's footsteps as a nature writer:

1. Visit a city park or a nearby field. You may want to do this with a partner.
2. Bring a small notebook and a pencil with you. A pencil is better than a pen so you can make some sketches.
3. Walk about slowly and open all your senses. If you see a tree, do you also hear birdsongs? How do the bark and leaves feel?
4. Take note of the season and the weather. Is it windy, chilly, sunny, rainy? There is no bad time to keep a journal.
5. Look for, and record observations of trees, weeds, wildflowers, insects, birds, and other wildlife.
6. Include your thoughts and feelings with what you observe.
7. Write spontaneously. Include poetry if you like. Don't worry right now about complete sentences.
8. Draw pictures on pages between your writing. Or press leaves or flowers between the pages.
9. Have fun.

▲▼ John continued to sketch sights in the wilderness throughout his California years. Half Dome rock (above) is perhaps the most recognizable image of Yosemite. That's the Half Dome on the back of the California state quarter (see page 41). Below is his sketch of a Western Juniper, a tree that can grow at altitudes as high as 10,000 feet (3,000 m).

the Native people of Alaska. John admired the spiritual bond between Native people and nature. He admired their lifestyles and knowledge of the wilderness, but his brand of preservation, like his father's religion, was very strict. He believed that everyone must leave nature's wilderness as pure as they found it. And because Native Americans left a faint mark, John argued they should not be allowed to live in national parks.

Earlier in his life, during his 1,000-mile walk, John expressed similar views of the former slaves he met. John was an environmental visionary, but it sometimes seemed that often he valued plant life, animal life, and even rocks, more than he did people.

A Man of Determination

Before John had his famous camping trip with President Roosevelt, his early essays opened the eyes of President Grover Cleveland. Cleveland declared 21 million acres (8.5 million hectares) of woodland as federal forest reserves. He also set in motion legislation to establish Yosemite, Sequoia, and Grand Canyon National Parks. These parks were opposed by many business people and industrial leaders with friends in the government. But conservationists won when Congress buckled under public support fueled by a barrage of John's fiery magazine articles.

The fight for Yosemite was dearest to John's heart and soul. Even after Yosemite achieved national park status, its meadows and hillsides were still used for grazing by commercial sheep ranchers. By then, John believed that trees and mountains were holy. His devotion to the wilderness was almost religious, and he saw industry, ranchers, and anyone who disturbed the purity of nature as if they were nonbelievers. He had to stop them. This was his mission.

John published another flurry of magazine articles, but this time his efforts were not a complete success. Many conservationists supported controlled grazing in the park, but John saw any grazing as overgrazing, a blight on his holy land.

Playing Hardball

John knew he needed more muscle, and in 1892 he organized and founded the Sierra Club. The Club took it upon itself to police the ranchers and their herds. Members also pressured state and the national governments to protect Yosemite and other areas by law. John was the club's president, and he set the agenda.

Within Yosemite was a special area called Hetch Hetchy Valley. To John, it was the most beautiful and sacred area he had ever walked. "No holier temple has ever been consecrated," he wrote. Although it was a protected area, the booming city of San Francisco badly needed a reservoir to provide clean water and generate electricity. In 1901, San

▲ John fought to close protected lands to sheep herders. He saw first hand how quickly a large herd of sheep could reduce a meadow of flowers and grasses to a dry, dusty field of dirt.

◄ John Muir founded The Sierra Club in 1892 to support his preservation plans. Here John and other members gather at Porcupine Flats, which today is one of Yosemite's most remote and rugged campsites.

John Muir fought a vehement but losing battle to stop construction of a dam that would flood Hetch Hetchy Valley. Above is a photo showing Hetch Hetchy just before it was flooded, and below, is one that shows Hetch Hetchy as it is today.

Francisco Mayor James Phelan proposed a plan to dam up the Toulumne River and flood Hetch Hetchy Valley.

Phelan, a conservationist, argued that public welfare, or the good of the people, outweighed preservation. As committed preservationists, John and the Sierra Club would not compromise. John called Phelan "Satan," and their battle raged for 12 years. The tragic San Francisco earthquake in 1906 heightened the dire need for a reservoir. John exerted his influence over William Howard Taft, president after Teddy Roosevelt, but when Woodrow Wilson was elected president after Taft, he signed the dam bill on December 19, 1913. Soon after, Hetch Hetchy Valley was an artificial lake.

John Muir's last battle—the fight to save the valley from flooding—ended in defeat. And there the battle would end. He died of pneumonia on December 24 of the following year, 1914, at the age of 76.

Chapter 5

The Legacy and Struggles Continue

Under cover of night, a small helicopter with bright searchlights hovers over a rudely cleared field deep in the protected land of Sequoia National Forest, in California at the southern end of the Sierra Nevada mountain range. As soon as the chopper lands, six men with large burlap bags rush under the whirling blades and load it up. It takes off just as quickly as it lands. Inside each bag are pounds of compact marijuana.

A Problem with Pollution

Scenes such as this have taken place thousands of times in recent years. Between 2007 and 2008 alone, the United States Forest Service discovered more than 700 marijuana farms in Sequoia alone. The farms are large and run by an organized and heavily armed criminal group called a drug cartel. In addition to contributing to drug and law enforcement problems, these farms use weed and bug sprays, rat poison, and plant growth hormones. Plastic pipes are used to siphon water to irrigate the plants, and pollutants flow back into streams and find their way into the drinking water for cities nearby. The Forest Service has called this a "crisis."

Another threat to national parks today is "spillover" pollution. This is pollution from unregulated areas that travels far beyond the

▲ Clean-up efforts such as this have used special agents and helicopters to remove thousands of plants and tons of equipment left behind by outlaw marijuana farmers.

"*Any fool can destroy trees. They (trees) cannot run away; and if they could, they would still be destroyed—chased and hunted down as long as fun or a dollar could be got out of their bark hides, branching horns, or magnificent bole backbones...*

Through all the wonderful, eventful centuries God has cared for these trees, saved them from drought, disease, avalanches, and a thousand straining, leveling tempests and floods; but he (sic) cannot save them from fools—only Uncle Sam can do that."

- John Muir. Found among Muir's papers after his death (first published by the Sierra Club, 1920)

▲▶ Despite growing environmental awareness, a few rude campers and irresponsible businesses still jeopardize wildlife in our National Parks.

site of pollution to spoil the natural beauty in the parks. For example, air pollution from automobiles is not just a city problem. Smog cannot be stopped from flowing to the air in the parks, endangering plant and animal life, and dimming the view of the night skies.

The biggest threat to the natural beauty and health of national parks comes from careless and inconsiderate campers. Inconsiderate campers leave behind non-biodegradable litter such as waxy candy wrappers, soda cans, chewed bubble gum, filter cigarette butts, plastic soda rings on the ground, and worse. Although most campers respect parks and honor park regulations, it only takes a few to undo John Muir's work by leaving behind litter or taking home plants, artifacts from archaeological sites, or even captured animals.

A Century of "Progress?"

It has been nearly 100 years since John Muir's death in 1914. Since then, environmental issues have become far more dangerous and far more complex. John Muir's followers today realize that there will be no national parks to protect if people don't stop and reverse toxic threats to the water, atmosphere, and entire planet. Many of these threats, such as global warming, were not even noticed until the danger loomed large. The need to respond is urgent, and responses must be smart.

Most scientists now agree that slowing down and reversing pollution on a global scale will require some major changes in the way we live. This means changing how we grow and package our food, how we heat and light our homes, and how we design and fuel our cars.

It won't be simple. Most businesses are tooled to make products and supply services that support the way we have lived for years. But that lifestyle helped make the environmental pollution of today. If we all stop drinking from plastic bottles tomorrow, what happens to the plastic bottle company? What happens to the jobs at the plastic bottle company? What happens to the families who

> "A tree is a tree. How many more do you need to look at."
>
> - Ronald Reagan, 40th president of the United States (spoken while a candidate for governor of California)

◀ Our whole world is one interconnected environment. Car exhaust is not just a city problem. Air pollution harms plants and other wildlife everywhere.

A Subject for Debate

Ask your teacher or debate coach to help you organize a class debate on the following Alberta oil field issue: The Alberta Oil Sand project is good for North America. Put three classmates on the "pro," or "yes," side and three others on the "con," or "no," side. Allow each debater three minutes to present his or her case. Then let the rest of the class decide. Debaters should be judged not by whether or not you agree with their position, but by how well each team presents its case.

▼ Much of the wilderness of Western Canada has been sacrificed in the name of the demand for oil. Scenes such as this outrage environmentalists and strengthen their calls for clean sources of energy.

depend on the paychecks from those jobs? There is more controversy and debate. Some argue that global warming is not "real," or that it is a normal part of nature's plan for some animals to become extinct.

For John Muir's followers, there have been setbacks and controversies. Today we live in a world that needs more oil than did the world of John Muir. In Alberta, Canada, there is a vast forest of spruce, pine, and aspen. This lush forest, about the size of Florida, sits on one of the world's richest supplies of oil known as the Alberta Oil Sands.

More than one million barrels of oil are extracted from these sands each day. This is more oil than comes from Venezuela, Russia, or Iran. When oil prices are high enough, many of the largest oil corporations in the United States and Canada work these fields around the clock to produce as much oil as they can. To make this possible, the Canadian government erased its signature from an international agreement on environmental protection known as the Kyoto Protocol.

The Great Debate

The benefits of extracting oil from these fields are enormous. It is a huge economic boon for the province of Alberta and all of Canada. It creates thousands of jobs. A high school graduate can earn $100,000 a year in the oil industry! Almost half of all Canada's oil is produced from these sands, and it all goes to the United States and Canada. The Organization of Petroleum Exporting Countries (OPEC) is a group of 12 oil-rich countries. They control about two-thirds of the world's oil reserves. Countries that use the most oil, including the United States, do not like to depend on these countries. The oil from Alberta Sands would help them get out of the OPEC headlock.

On the negative side, oil is not extracted from the Alberta Sands by drilling, but by water pressure. At the end of the process, the water is sludgy and polluted, and it is dumped into large artificial lakes of toxic waste. The extraction process also burns more natural gas than it takes to heat the chilly city of Calgary for a year. The operation has doubled Canada's greenhouse emissions, damaging the atmosphere and contributing to global warming. The pollution and contamination threaten Alberta's forests and rivers, as well as the towns of First Nations people and others as far as 175 miles (280 km) away.

Arguments boil on both sides of the issue. Some local and national officials in the United States refuse to take Alberta oil. Others argue that

▲ Extraction of oil creates artificial lakes of oily waste that can kill migrating birds that land there. Here workers set up giant scarecrows in hopes of preventing that from happening.

refusing Alberta oil makes the United States too dependent on oil from the Middle East and weakens United States security. The oil companies promise to develop pollution-reducing safeguards on their own, but David Suzuki, Canada's leading environmental activist, argues that oil companies cannot be trusted, and government laws are needed. Politicians are divided, with some supporting the oil project and others opposing it. The same issues surround offshore drilling, commercial farming, and other environmental hot topics. The debate rages on.

In the Footsteps of John Muir— Environmental Activism

If environmental threats have become more menacing and opposition to environmentalism has been flexing its muscles, so has the activism that began with John Muir. No longer a few voices in the wilderness, environmentalism has organized. The Sierra Club has expanded its mission, and newer organizations such as the World Wildlife Fund and Greenpeace and have joined the movement.

The Sierra Club still follows its original mission of preserving wilderness. One current priority is the

▼   Today, members of area Sierra Club chapters often work on local cleanup projects. This volunteer crew cleared more than 500 tires and other pieces of debris from San Francisco Bay during low tide. When they were done, trucks and helicopters transported the trash to the city dump.

Club's active opposition to oil and gas drilling along the coasts and in the Arctic National Wildlife Refuge. The Sierra Club also uses education programs and publications to work on awareness of its number one issue, global warming. Its members advocate the use of wind and solar energy as alternatives to fossil fuels and nuclear power. The Club's third priority is to educate the public to the alarming accumulation of toxic mercury found in children.

The World Wildlife Fund, which was founded in Switzerland in 1961, is now the world's largest conservation group, with more than five million members. In 2008, the WWF (as it is more commonly known), issued a scathing report blaming "reckless consumption" as the most dangerous threat to our planet. By reckless consumption, the WWF means using up natural resources faster than those resources can be renewed by nature. An individual's or country's depletion of resources is sometimes known as its ecological footprint.

The WWF lists the five countries with the largest rates of reckless consumption as the United Arab Emirates, the United States, Kuwait, Denmark, and Australia. The countries with the smallest rate include Haiti, Congo, Bangladesh,

◄ It is estimated that as many as 40 percent of all species are endangered. The World Wildlife Fund is dedicated to saving endangered species such as blue whales, snow leopards, and polar bears.

Malawi, and Afghanistan, but these are also countries where life for the average citizen is filled with hardship. Clearly there needs to be a balance. Many developed countries must reduce their depletion of resources while many underdeveloped countries deserve to use more resources responsibly to improve their quality of life. The WWF remains equally committed to its original, 1960s mission of identifying and saving endangered species.

Greenpeace is an international organization with almost three million members and 30 chapters around the world. Greenpeace champions many of the same issues as the Sierra Club and the WWF, but its tactics go beyond education and lobbying into acts of protest and defiance. Some Greenpeace protests take the form of civil disobedience. The concept of civil disobedience was developed by the American writer Henry David Thoreau, who influenced John Muir and other activists, such as Martin Luther King, Jr. People who practice civil disobedience protest laws and practices by opposing those laws with non-violent actions.

In 2008, members of Greenpeace Canada chained themselves to the entrance of Canada's largest logging company. They did this to draw attention to the company's practice of deforestation, which threatens the biodiversity of the Boreal Forest, even though it meant they would be arrested.

▲ Environmental groups such as Greenpeace have recently expanded both their mission and their tactics. Here Greenpeace members chain themselves to a huge ship carrying genetically modified livestock food.

Some Greenpeace actions go beyond civil disobedience, however, and they have been accused of eco-terrorism. Greenpeace owns a fleet of ships. They have used these vessels to chase down and threaten to ram commercial whaling and tuna ships.

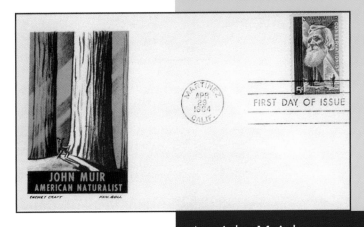

Honors and Accolades for a Life Well Lived

Since his death, John Muir has been accorded many honors, often in ways that go beyond bestowing a medal or issuing a proclamation.

In 1980, a musical extravaganza based on the life of John Muir premiered. *Mountain Days* features a cast of 85. It depicts Muir's boyhood, his 1,000-mile walk, his travels in Yosemite, and his evolution from naturalist to crusader in his quest to preserve natural lands of beauty for future generations.

In 1988, Congress officially declared April 21 as John Muir Day. In California, schools use the day to study his life and work.

In 2004, an asteroid outside the orbit of Mars was discovered. It is less than a mile (1.6 km) across—large enough to be described as a planetoid or minor planet—and its discoverer named it "Johnmuir."

In 2006 John Muir was inducted into the California Hall of Fame. He now stands with other California celebrities and heroes such as Dr. Seuss, Willie Mays, Jackie Robinson, Tiger Woods, Amelia Earhart, Cesar Chavez, and others.

▲ John Muir has been featured on a United States coin and two United States postage stamps: the 2005 "California" state quarter, a 1964 five-cent first class stamp (both shown here) and a 1998 32-cent first class stamp.

▲ Petrified trees are trees whose trunks have become fossilized, or turned into stone. John Muir helped establish the National Petrified Forest in Arizona.

The Legacy Lives On

From his 1,000-mile walk to his fight to save Hetch Hetchy, John Muir's legacy lives on. His fight to protect nature remains as relevant and inspirational today as it was 100–150 years ago. Global warming, energy independence, and even national security depend on the preservation and respect for nature that Muir exemplified his entire life. His life is proof that one person can make a difference. As a writer and crusader, he helped establish many of the grandest national parks in the United States, including Grand Canyon National Park, the Petrified Forest, and Yosemite. He influenced presidents and the United States Congress to pass laws protecting the natural landmarks from people who wanted to use those lands for personal profit. He founded the Sierra Club, which continues to be a leading voice for conservation and environmental protection today. And his legacy inspires people to recycle, conserve energy, support environmental groups, and understand and feel the connection with all of nature.

The biggest honor of all is that John Muir's work is being carried on to this day.

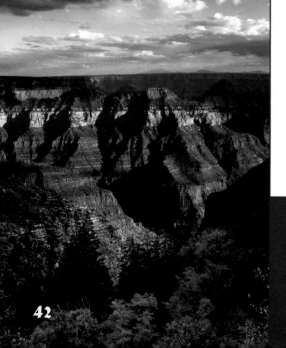

◄ The Grand Canyon was "carved" out by the Colorado River over the course of six million years. The preservation efforts of President Theodore Roosevelt and John Muir helped ensure that this magnificent work will not be undone.

Chronology

1838	April 21, John Muir is born in Dunbar, Scotland
1849	Immigrates with some family members to Wisconsin at the age of 11
1860	Exhibits inventions at the Wisconsin State Fair
1861–1862	Attends the University of Wisconsin for two and a half years
1863	Leaves the university to walk and work in Canada
1867	Suffers an eye injury while working in an Indianapolis factory. Begins 1,000-mile walk to Florida
1868	Voyages to California. Lands in San Francisco, March 28 and walks across the Yosemite Valley
1872	Begins to publish articles in leading magazines
1879	Takes first trip to Alaska; discovers Glacier Bay and Muir Glacier
1880	On April 14 marries Louisa Strentzel (33); takes second trip to Alaska
1881	Daughter Wanda is born; takes third trip to Alaska aboard the *Corwin*
1882	Begins extensive ranching period
1886	Daughter Helen is born
1888	Takes trip to Mt. Rainier; contributes to *Picturesque California*
1890	Yosemite becomes a national park
1892	The Sierra Club is founded
1899	Mt. Rainier National Park established
1901	*Our National Parks* is published
1902–1913	Fights to save Hetch Hetchy Valley in Yosemite
1903	Camps with President Theodore Roosevelt in Yosemite
1904	Takes a world tour
1905	Wife Louisa dies on August 6
1906	Petrified Forest becomes a national monument
1908	Grand Canyon National Park is established
1909–1913	*Stickeen* (1909), *My First Summer in the Sierra* (1911), *The Yosemite* (1912), and *The Story of My Boyhood and Youth* (1913) are published
1911–1912	Travels to South America and Africa at the age of 73
1914	On December 24, dies of pneumonia in a Los Angeles Hospital
1916	Congress creates National Park Service
1989	April 21 is proclaimed John Muir Day by California Governor George Deukmejian
2006	John Muir is inducted into the California Hall of Fame by Governor Arnold Schwarzenegger

Glossary

biodegradable waste Trash that can rot or decompose. It takes an orange peel one month to biodegrade; six-pack plastic holders can take 450 years. Foam cups may never biodegrade

biodiversity The number of different plants and animals found in an area. Pollution and deforestation can disturb an area's biodiversity

biome A large geographical area of plant and animal groups that have adapted to the area's environment. Major biomes include deserts, forests, grasslands, tundra, as well as oceans and waterways

botany The scientific study of plant life. Biology may be divided into botany and zoology, the study of animals

civil disobedience The act of refusing to obey a law through peaceful and nonviolent acts. The intention is to change a governmental policy because it is morally wrong, and to accept the consequences, even if it means a fine or going to jail. The term was first used in 1849 by American nature writer Henry David Thoreau when he protested the Mexican-American War by refusing to pay taxes

conservationist Someone who believes in the responsible use and protection of nature for the public good

deforestation Removing trees from a forest by cutting down or burning. Deforestation can lead to erosion, drought, loss of biodiversity through extinction of plant and animal species, and increased levels of carbon dioxide and other greenhouse gases. Many nations have undertaken reforestation to reverse the effects of deforestation

eco-terrorism Destruction or the threat of destruction of the property of individuals and groups who endanger the environment

foothills Low hills at the base of a mountain or mountain range

ford To cross (usually a river) at a shallow point

geology The scientific study of rocks, rock formations, and mountains that shape Earth's crust

greenhouse gases Gases in the atmosphere that keep Earth warm. The four main greenhouse gases are carbon dioxide, methane, nitrous oxide, and fluorocarbons. Global warming occurs when there is an increase in greenhouse gases. The results of global warming include severe floods and droughts, huge swarms of insects, and other disruptions to the environment

Greenpeace An international organization founded in 1971 and dedicated to stopping the threat of global warming, deforestation, deterioration of the oceans, and the threat of a nuclear disaster

Kyoto Protocol An international agreement dedicated to the reduction of carbon dioxide and other greenhouse gases. Each country in the agreement must keep its carbon dioxide emissions below an assigned level. Both the United States and Canada first signed and then later withdrew from the agreement

naturalist Someone who studies or is an expert in nature and natural history

OPEC The Organization of Petroleum Exporting Countries, a group of countries that attempt to regulate the supply and price of oil they sell. As of 2008 there are 12 members. The five founding countries are Iran, Iraq, Kuwait, Saudi Arabia, and Venezuela

ornithologist A person who specializes in the scientific study of birds

pacificism The belief that war and violence are never justified to settle disputes

parasite An organism, or living thing, that lives on or in another organism, called a host, and gets its nutrition from that other organism

preservationist Someone who believes that nature should not be disturbed or changed by people under any circumstances

rambunctious Lively, active, and boisterous; often uncontrollably so

renewable resources Materials that can be used for energy without depleting the supply. When wind and solar power provide energy, they do not use up wind or sunshine. Wood can be a renewable resource only if it is used at the same or lesser rate than it takes to grow more trees

Sierra Club Organization founded by John Muir in 1892 to preserve the wilderness, particularly Hetch Hetchy Valley, from industrial development. Today the Club's mission has four parts. "Explore, enjoy, and protect the wild places of the earth. Practice and promote the responsible use of the earth's ecosystems and resources. Educate and enlist humanity to protect and restore the quality of the natural and human environment. Use all lawful means to carry out these objectives"

topography A detailed study and description of the surface of a land and water area. More than just a map, topography records the height and depth of an area's meadows, mountains, cliffs, canyons, fields, forests, and waterways

transcendentalism A belief that life's big truths can only be learned through nature at unexpected moments. In the 1800s, writers Ralph Waldo Emerson and Henry David Thoreau helped explain and promote these beliefs. They were a strong influence on John Muir

Further Information

Books

Aretha, David. *Yellowstone National Park* (America's National Parks). Enslow Publishers, 2009.

Bishop, Amanda. *Reducing Your Carbon Footprint* (Energy Revolution). Crabtree Publishing, 2008.

Byrnes, Patricia. *Environmental Pioneers*. The Oliver Press, 1998.

Connolly, Sean. *Greenpeace* (Global Organizations). Smart Apple Media, 2009.

Dunlap, Julie and Marybeth Lorbiecki. *John Muir and Stickeen: An Icy Adventure with a No-Good Dog*. NorthWord Press, 2004.

Web sites

www.greenpeace.org/usa/
www.greenpeace.org/canada/en/
The official sites for Greenpeace USA and Greenpeace Canada feature changing articles on current news, photos, video, and message boards.

www.kidsface.org/
Kids For a Clean Environment (FACE) has 300,000 members worldwide. Its mission is "recycle, build, plant." The site has information about student projects.

www.kidsforsavingearth.org
Kids for Saving Earth (KSE) provides educational materials, posters, certificates, guidebooks, CDs, and information to kids, families, groups, classrooms, and schools. The mission of KSE is to educate, inspire, and empower children to protect Earth's environment.

www.sierraclub.org/
The official site of the Sierra Club has links to information about its founder, John Muir, as well as suggestions for John Muir Day classroom projects. The site also contains a link for a Spanish-language version of the Web site.

www.nps.gov/
The site of the National Parks Service has information about each national park.

www.worldwildlife.org/
The home site of the World Wildlife Fund (WWF) is complete with links to photos, eCards, screensavers, and articles about endangered species throughout the world.

Index

About the Author

Henry Elliot lives in Pittsburgh. He is active in neighborhood restoration projects, and he spends much time walking along the banks of Pittsburgh's three rivers, the Allegheny, the Monongahela, and the Ohio.

Printed in the U.S.A. — CG